Apes and Monkeys

KINGFISHER
LONDON & NEW YORK

Copyright © Macmillan Children's Books 2011
Published in the United States by Kingfisher,
175 Fifth Ave., New York, NY 10010
Kingfisher is an imprint of Macmillan Children's Books, London.
All rights reserved.

Distributed in the U.S. by Macmillan, 175 Fifth Ave., New York, NY 10010

First published as *Kingfisher Young Knowledge: Apes and Monkeys* in 2004
Additional material produced for Kingfisher by Discovery Books Ltd.

Library of Congress Cataloging-in-Publication data has been applied for.

ISBN: 978-0-7534-6603-2

Kingfisher books are available for special promotions and premiums. For details contact: Special
Markets Department, Macmillan, 175 Fifth Ave., New York, NY 10010.

For more information, please visit www.kingfisherbooks.com

Printed in China
1 3 5 7 9 8 6 4 2
1TR/0511/WKT/UG/140MA

Acknowledgments
The publisher would like to thank the following for permission to reproduce their material. Every care has been taken
to trace copyright holders. However, if there have been unintentional omissions or failure to trace copyright holders,
we apologize and will, if informed, endeavor to make corrections in any future edition.
b = bottom, *c* = center, *l* = left, *t* = top, *r* = right

Photographs: *cover* Shutterstock Images; 4–5 Steve Bloom; 6–7 Oxford Scientific Films; 8 Martin
Harvey/NHPA; 9 Ardea; 10–11 Ardea; 11*tl* Oxford Scientific Films; 12*br* Oxford Scientific Films; 13*tl* Oxford
Scientific Films; 14 Ardea; 15*t* Rojer Eritja/Alamy; 15*b* Steve Bloom; 16 Oxford Scientific Films; 17 Steve
Bloom; 18*b* Anup Shah/Nature Picture Library; 20*tr* Oxford Scientific Films; 22*b* Steve Bloom; 23*tr* Peter
Blackwell/Nature Picture Library; 23*l* Art Wolfe/Getty Images; 23*br* James Warwick/NHPA; 24*bl* Ardea;
24–25 Steve Bloom; 25*br* Ardea; 26*bl* Kevin Schafer/Corbis; 26*t* Tony Hamblin/Corbis; 29 Mark
Bowler/NHPA; 30–31*b* Richard du Toit/NHPA; 31*tl* Anup Shah/Nature Picture Library; 31 Roland Seitre/Still
Pictures; 32*bl* Oxford Scientific Films; 32*br* Ardea; 33*tl* Oxford Scientific Films; 33*r* Anup Shah/Nature
Picture Library; 34*bl* Theo Allofs/Corbis; 34*r* Ardea; 35 Steve Bloom; 36*b* Anup Shah/Nature Picture Library;
36*t* Getty Images; 37*tl* Dietmar Nill/Nature Picture Library; 37*b* Frank Lane Picture Agency;
38*b* Anup Shah/Nature Picture Library; 38*t* Ardea; 39 Getty Images; 40*tl* Ardea; 40*b* Karl Ammann/Nature
Picture Library; 41 Ardea; 48*t* Shutterstock Images/Cloudia Newland; 48*b* Shutterstock Images/Stéphane
Bidouze; 49*l* Shutterstock Images/Jackiso; 49*r* Shutterstock Images/Anan Kaewkhammul;
52*l* Shutterstock Images/Bernhard Richter; 52*r* Shutterstock Images/Stacey Bates; 53 Shutterstock
Images/namatae; 56 Shutterstock Images/Mertens Photography

Commissioned photography on pages 42–47 by Andy Crawford
Thank you to models Aaron Hibbert, Lewis Manu, Alastair Roper, and Rebecca Roper

Apes and Monkeys

Barbara Taylor

KINGFISHER
NEW YORK

Contents

What is an ape?

You are one! There are four other great apes—gorillas, chimpanzees (chimps), orangutans, and bonobos. Gibbons are small apes. Apes have gripping fingers and thumbs and no tail.

Hairy apes

Apes are a kind of mammal, which is an animal with a hairy body. Hair helps keep mammals warm. We have much less hair than the other apes, such as this gorilla.

Brainy apes

All apes have a big brain and are intelligent. They can solve problems, use tools, remember things, and communicate with one another. Humans are the only apes that can speak.

Arms and legs

Most apes' arms are longer than their legs. They can swing through the trees or walk on all fours. Humans walk upright on long legs.

Apes in Africa

Three types of big wild apes live in the forests, woodlands, and mountains of Africa. These are gorillas, bonobos, and chimps. They all live in large groups.

Gorilla groups

Gorillas live in peaceful groups of between five and 20 members. The group of males, females, and young is led by a big male.

bonobo   *chimpanzee*

Girl power

Bonobos look like chimps but are more graceful. They have smaller heads and ears and longer legs than chimps. Female bonobos lead the groups.

Noisy chimpanzees

Chimps live in the biggest groups, with up to 100 members. A few important male chimps lead each group. Chimps are noisier and fight more often than the other African apes.

Apes in Asia

Orangutans and gibbons are apes that live in Asia. They spend a lot of time in trees, although sometimes male orangutans have to climb down, as they grow too big for the branches.

Fatty faces

Male orangutans have fatty pads the size of dinner plates on their faces. These make them look bigger and help them scare away any rivals.

Singing apes

Siamang gibbons are the
biggest of the gibbons. They
sing to tell other gibbons where
they live. Pouches on their throats
inflate as they sing, making
their voices even louder.

Getting around

Chimpanzees and gorillas spend a lot of time on the ground. Orangutans, gibbons, and bonobos climb in the trees. Gibbons live high in the treetops.

Knuckle walking

When chimps walk on all fours, they rest their weight on thick pads of skin on their knuckles.

Swinging apes

Gibbons swing from branch to branch using first one hand and then the other. They can move very quickly without making much noise.

Hanging on

Orangutans grip onto branches tightly with their long, hooked fingers. Their arms can stretch a long way. Each arm is almost twice as long as each leg!

Finding food

Apes feed mostly on fruit and leaves, but they also eat a small amount of meat, such as insects. Chimps sometimes eat larger animals, including monkeys.

Going fishing!

Chimps chew sticks or grass stems to make them the right shape to dig for food. They then push the sticks into a termite mound. When they pull them out, termites are clinging to the end.

Fruit feast

Durian is one of the orangutan's favorite foods. They remember where to find trees with ripe fruit.

Tasty termites

Millions of termites live
inside a termite mound.
They can provide a tasty
snack for hungry
chimpanzees.

Brainy apes

Apes are one of the few animals to make and use tools, which is one sign of an intelligent animal.

Tough nuts to crack

Some chimps bang a heavy stone onto nuts. This works like a hammer and cracks open their hard shells.

Rainy days

Apes do not like the rain because their fur is not very waterproof. This orangutan has made its own umbrella out of bark.

Chatty chimps

The chimpanzees in a group make different sounds, make faces, and use the position of their bodies to "talk" to their family and friends.

Making faces

With their big eyes and flexible lips, chimps are good at making faces. Their expressions show how they are feeling.

Playtime

As young chimps play, they learn how to mix with other chimps in their group. They also learn which chimps are the most important in the group.

Sound signals

Chimps use their big ears
to listen for sounds drifting
through the forest. The
members of a group
hoot to one another
to stay in touch.

Forever friends

Chimps may have special
friends within their group.
These friends hug each
other for comfort and
to show that they
are still friends.

Baby apes

Apes usually have one baby at a time. They spend many years teaching the baby how to move, feed, and behave.

Gibbon families

Gibbons live in small family groups. A gibbon father plays with his baby and helps take care of it.

Riding piggyback

Many baby apes, such as this gorilla, are carried around until they are strong enough to walk by themselves.

Motherly love
A baby orangutan lives with its mother for seven to nine years. It does not usually have any other playmates.

What is a monkey?

A monkey is an intelligent, playful mammal with a tail. It usually lives in groups for safety. There are 130 different monkeys, from tiny tamarins to big baboons.

Living quarters

Monkeys live in a wide range of habitats, from forests and mountains to grasslands and swamps. These proboscis monkeys live in a swamp.

Terrific tails

Monkey tails can be long or short, thick or thin, and straight or curly. This colobus uses its fluffy tail to steer as it leaps through the trees.

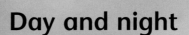

Day and night

The owl monkey is the only monkey that comes out at night. It has big eyes to help it see in the dark.

Brainiac

Capuchins are intelligent monkeys with a large brain. This helps them live in a range of different habitats.

American monkeys

American monkeys live in the warm rainforests of Central and South America. They have wide, round nostrils that are far apart. Many have prehensile tails, which are tails that grip like an extra hand.

Finger food
Tamarins have long fingers, which they use to search for their insect food. They have claws instead of fingernails.

Treetop leapers

Little squirrel monkeys leap through the trees like squirrels and climb onto thin branches. They live in big groups of up to 200 monkeys.

Furry monkeys

Saki monkeys have long, shaggy fur, which helps protect them from heavy rain. They may suck water off their fur.

African and Asian monkeys

These monkeys have nostrils that are close together and hard pads on their bottoms to help them sleep sitting up. They do not have prehensile tails.

Packed lunch
The red-tailed monkey stores its food in cheek pouches and then finds a safe place to sit and eat.

Follow the leader
Slim, graceful mona monkeys live in troops of up to 20 monkeys. Each troop is led by a strong male. Monas have striking marks and colors on their soft, thick fur.

Hot baths

Japanese macaques live in the mountains. In the cold, snowy winter, they grow thick coats and sit in hot spring water to keep warm.

Spot the difference?

Monkeys are smaller than apes and not as intelligent. Monkeys usually have a tail, but apes never have a tail.

Big ape

Gorillas are the biggest of the wild apes. Female gorillas weigh about half as much as males. The size of the males scares off predators and rivals.

Monkey tails
The spider monkey curls its prehensile tail around branches. The bare, ridged skin under the tail helps it cling tightly.

Moving and grooving

Monkeys scamper along the tops of branches or run fast along the ground. They do not usually swing through the branches, like apes do.

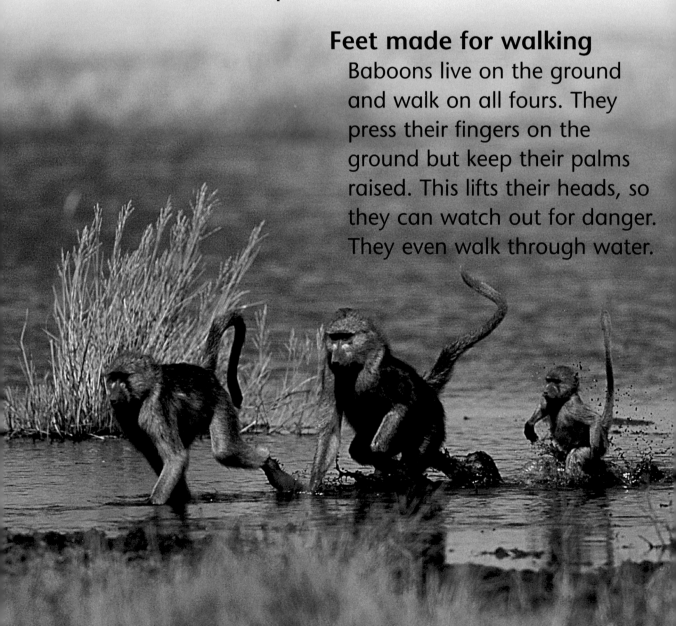

Feet made for walking

Baboons live on the ground and walk on all fours. They press their fingers on the ground but keep their palms raised. This lifts their heads, so they can watch out for danger. They even walk through water.

Leggy leapers

The long back legs of colobus monkeys help them push off strongly from branches. They can make huge leaps from tree to tree.

Hanging around

Uakaris live at the tops of tall trees in swampy and flooded forests. They sometimes use their powerful back legs to hang upside down.

Hungry monkeys

A monkey's favorite food is usually fruit. Monkeys also feed on leaves, nuts, flowers, and insects. Some have special diets, such as the marmosets that eat tree gum.

Nuts and seeds

Sakis spend a lot of time eating seeds. Some sakis have strong jaws to crack open hard nuts and reach the soft food that is stored inside.

Clever capuchin

This capuchin is chewing bark from a small branch. It can also crack open nuts or shells by hitting them on rocks.

Meat for dinner

Baboons are strong, smart, and agile enough to catch other monkeys, birds, and small antelope.

Green salad

Colobus monkeys mostly eat leaves, but they also enjoy munching on ripe fruit, flowers, and seeds. Bacteria in their big stomachs release energy from their food.

Getting to know you

Monkeys have many ways of staying in touch. They also use calls, colors, and behavior to find a mate and to warn of danger.

Stay away!

Howlers are the world's noisiest land animals! Their calls warn other howlers to stay away.

Bad hair day?

Monkeys and apes groom each other's fur. They pick out any dirt or bugs they find and clean up any scratches. Grooming helps monkeys stay clean and remain friends.

Color signals

The colors of the male mandrill become brighter when he is healthy, angry, or excited. Females prefer males with bright colors.

Baby monkeys

Monkey mothers take care of their babies until they are about 12 to 18 months old— a shorter time than apes.

New babies

Baby monkeys have their eyes open at birth and can cling onto their mother's fur.

Babysitting

Langur mothers let other females hold and take care of their babies. This makes their lives easier.

Mother's milk

Like other mammals, vervet monkey mothers make milk in their bodies to feed their babies. They have to eat a lot of food to give them enough energy to make this milk.

Watch with mother

Monkey babies, like this spider monkey, cling onto their mothers. They watch the other monkeys in the troop to learn how to climb and leap, which food is good to eat, and how to behave.

Apes and monkeys in danger

All the apes (except humans) and many monkeys are in danger of becoming extinct. The main reason for this is humans.

Ape crisis

Some of the apes, including the white-handed gibbon seen here, could be extinct in only 20 years. We must do more to protect them from hunting and habitat destruction.

Disappearing act

Marmosets, like this tufted-ear marmoset, have lost their forest homes. They are also caught and sold as pets.

Monkey madness

The rare Chinese golden monkey is threatened by hunting for its meat and fur. The trees in its forest home are also being cut down.

Saving apes and monkeys

We can help save apes and monkeys by protecting their habitats, breeding rare ones in zoos, and finding ways for people and wild animals to live together.

Special survivor

Golden lion tamarins have been saved by protecting their forest homes in Brazil.

Finding out more

We need to find out more about apes and monkeys so that we can help them survive. Scientists such as Dr. Jane Goodall (right) study chimps and work to save them and their habitats.

Orphan apes

If a mother ape dies or is killed, her baby needs a lot of love and care. People sometimes look after these orphans and may one day release them back into the wild.

Monkey mobile

Make a monkey chain

Follow steps 1 to 5 to make one monkey. Then make more monkeys and hook their arms together in a long chain.

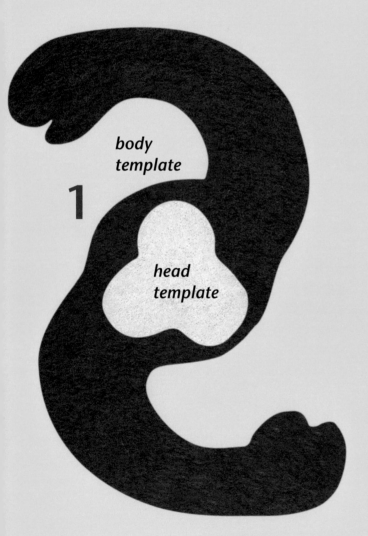

body template

1

head template

Trace the two templates with a pencil and transfer the outline shapes onto a paper plate.

2

Using the scissors, carefully cut out the cardboard templates. Hold the edge of the plate with one hand to stop it from moving.

3

Fold a piece of brown felt in half and secure it with a safety pin. Trace around the body template with a marker and then cut it out.

You will need:

- Tracing paper
- Pencil and black marker
- Paper plates
- Scissors
- Brown and tan felt
- Safety pin
- Glue

4

Glue the felt body shapes onto the back and front of the cardboard shapes. Make the faces out of tan felt and glue them on.

5

Cut out four small "D" shapes and glue them on as ears. Use a black marker to draw on the eyes, nose and mouth.

Termite towers

Eat like a chimpanzee

Make your own termite tower.
Then put food inside and use
a straw to get the food out.
It is not as easy as it looks!

You will need:

- Cardboard tubes
- Tape
- Scissors
- Paper plate
- Pencil
- Newspaper
- Glue or flour
- Water
- Paper towels
- Poster paints
- Paintbrush
- Candies
- Drinking straws

1 Find four clean cardboard tubes
and tape them together. Ask a
parent or friend to hold the
tubes still.

2 Turn a paper plate upside down.
Hold the four tubes over the
plate and draw around them
with a pencil.

3 Using the scissors, carefully cut
out the holes in the paper plate.
Then tape the tubes firmly in
place over the holes.

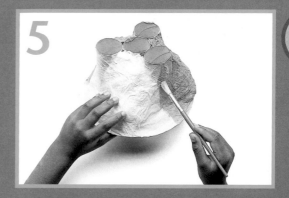

Scrunch up pieces of newspaper and stick them into the gaps between the tubes. This should make a mound shape.

Mix flour and water together (or use glue) to stick strips of paper towel and newspaper over the mound. Paint it to look like mud.

Choose some candies that are larger than the end of a straw and place them in the tubes. Suck through a straw to pull out the candies. How many can you catch?

Monkey masks

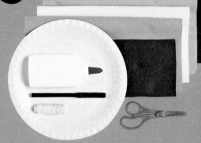

Make a monkey face

Monkeys and apes have round heads
that are perfect for making masks.
Find your favorite monkey or ape
in this book and make a mask of its face.

You will need:
- Felt-tip pen
- Tracing paper
- Colored felt
- Scissors
- Glue
- Paper plate
- Elastic

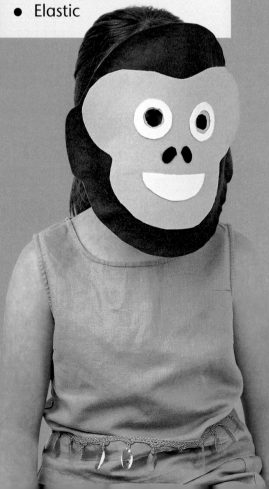

1

Draw the head of the monkey
onto tracing paper. Place it on
brown felt and carefully cut out
around the outside edges.

2

Trace the face shape of the
monkey onto tracing paper.
Put this over the tan felt and
cut it out.

Glue the tan felt on top of the brown felt and stick them both onto a paper plate. Glue white felt rings around the eyes.

Glue on a felt nose and mouth. Then cut out eye holes and tie or glue elastic to the sides of the mask to hold it on.

Glossary

bacteria—tiny, one-celled life forms

bonobo—a species of ape, similar to a chimpanzee but smaller

communicate—to make other animals understand your message

diet—the food an animal usually eats

DNA—deoxyribonucleic acid, the material that our genes are made of

durian—a large, very smelly fruit

expression—the "look" on a face

extinct—when an animal species has completely died out

forest—a very large area of trees

groom—to pick through fur with fingers

habitat—the area where an animal lives

inflate—to fill up with air

intelligent—smart and able to understand things easily

IQ—intelligence quotient, a measure of a person or animal's intelligence

knuckle—one of the joints where a finger bends

mammal—an animal that feeds its babies on mother's milk

orphan—having no mother or father

predator—an animal that hunts and eats other animals

prehensile tail—a tail that grips tightly

rival—a competitor for food or mates

tool—an object that helps with work

troop—a group of monkeys

The content of this book will be useful to help teach and reinforce various elements of the science and language arts curricula in the elementary grades. It also provides opportunities for crosscurricular lessons in geography, visual and performing arts, and math.

Extension activities

Writing
1) The image on p. 41 shows an orphaned baby ape clinging to the leg of a human caregiver. Write about what has happened to lead up to this photo using one of these styles:
• an article for a nature magazine
• a letter from the caregiver to a friend
• a diary entry written from the point of view of the baby ape

2) Most apes and monkeys are in danger of becoming extinct. One way to help is to let others know about this crisis. Research to learn more about why and how a particular ape or monkey is threatened. When you have all the facts, write a letter to your school or local newspaper to tell people about the danger and why it is important to protect these animals.

Literature
Look in the library for both fiction and nonfiction stories about monkeys and/or apes. Make a list of which characteristics are realistic and which are not.

Science
The topic of apes and monkeys relates to the scientific themes of behavior, diversity, adaptation, and the structure and function of conservation. Some specific links to science curriculum content include communication (pp. 11, 18–19, 34–35); evolution (p. 6); food chains and webs (pp. 14–15, 32–33); growth and development (pp. 20–21, 36–37); and predator/prey relationships and survival (pp. 14–15, 28–29, 33, 34–35).

Crosscurricular links

1) Writing, oral language, and geography: Choose a monkey or ape and write a one-page report about its life and habitat. Include a map showing where it lives. Share your information in a short oral report.

2) Geography, writing, and art: Three different types of gorillas live in Africa: western lowland, eastern lowland, and mountain gorillas. Draw a map of Africa, including a key to show where each type of gorilla is found. Describe the terrain using words and/or pictures. (This links with the topic of ecosystems and biomes.)

3) Math: Research to find the heights and weights of several different apes and monkeys. Make two graphs—one to compare heights and the other to compare weights.

Using the projects

Children can do these projects at home. Here are some ideas for extending them:

Pages 42–43: Use white felt or white construction paper instead of brown felt. Look at the illustrations of monkeys beginning on p. 22. Color each of the monkeys in your chain to represent the coloration of a different type of monkey.

Pages 46–47: Get together with some friends and write a play starring a group of monkeys. Act it out, wearing the masks that you have made.

Did you know?

- It is easy to tell the difference between apes and monkeys: monkeys have tails; apes do not.

- In zoos, young gorillas receive the same injections as human babies, because gorillas can pick up the same diseases as humans.

- Orangutans make a new nest in the trees every night to sleep in.

- Monkeys use their voice, facial expressions, and body movements to communicate.

- The smallest monkey in the world is the pygmy marmoset. It measures 4.6–6.3 inches (117–159 millimeters) and weighs 3–5 ounces (85–140 grams)—about as much as a cell phone!

- The howler monkey is the loudest monkey: its howls can be heard from about 2 miles (3 kilometers) away.

- Orangutans can live for up to 50 years in the wild.

- Gorillas are the largest living primates. They can grow to more than 6.5 feet (2 meters) tall and weigh up to 500 pounds (230 kilograms)—about the same as three men!

- When a monkey yawns, it usually means it is either tired or angry.

- Bonobos sometimes use sticks to defend themselves.

- Chimpanzees communicate in similar ways to humans: by hugging, kissing, holding hands, and tickling.

- Monkeys groom one another to show affection.

- Orangutans are some of the most intelligent primates and are able to use a variety of tools.

- Chimpanzees are the closest relative to humans: they share 98 percent of our DNA.

Apes and monkeys quiz

The answers to these questions can all be found by looking back through the book. See how many you get right. You can check your answers on page 56.

1) Why do male orangutans have fatty plates on either side of their face?
A—to make them look bigger and to scare away any rivals
B—to hear better
C—to attract a mate

2) Which is the biggest gibbon?
A—lar gibbon
B—silvery gibbon
C—siamang gibbon

3) How many different types of monkeys are there?
A—13
B—130
C—1,300

4) Which of these monkeys comes out only at night?
A—proboscis monkey
B—colobus monkey
C—owl monkey

5) What do colobus monkeys usually eat?
A—leaves
B—eggs
C—worms

6) What do marmosets eat?
A—tree gum
B—insects
C—fruit

7) How long does a baby orangutan live with its mother?
A—between seven and nine weeks
B—between seven and nine months
C—between seven and nine years

8) What does the colobus monkey use its tail for?
A—to steer as it leaps between trees
B—to protect itself
C—to clean itself

9) Why do saki monkeys have long, shaggy fur?
A—to protect them from hot sun
B—to protect them from heavy rain
C—to keep them warm

10) Where do Japanese macaques live?
A—in the desert
B—by the sea
C—in the mountains

11) What part of their hands do chimps use when they walk on all fours?
A—palms
B—knuckles
C—fingertips

12) Which is the only ape that can speak?
A—gorilla
B—human
C—orangutan

Books to read

Apes (Endangered!) by Carol Ellis, Marshall Cavendish Children's Books, 2010

Baboons (Amazing Animals) by Christina Wilsdon, Gareth Stevens Publishing, 2010

Gorillas (Living Wild) by Melissa Gish, Creative Education, 2011

Monkeys and Apes (100 Facts) by Camilla de la Bedoyere, Miles Kelly Publishing Ltd., 2010

Top 50 Reasons to Care About Great Apes: Animals in Peril by David Barker, Enslow Publishers, 2010

Who on Earth is Jane Goodall?: Guardian of Chimpanzees (Scientists Saving the Earth) by Victoria Guidi, Enslow Publishers, 2009

Places to visit

Houston Zoo, Houston, Texas
www.houstonzoo.org/Wortham/
Houston Zoo's Wortham World of Primates has a boardwalk and arboreal treehouse where visitors can observe the behavior of a wide range of threatened primates, from howler monkeys to golden lion tamarins.

Red Ape Reserve, Oregon Zoo, Portland, Oregon
www.oregonzoo.org/Exhibits/RedApeReserve/walkthrough.htm
Visit the Red Ape Reserve at Oregon Zoo and get nose-to-nose with orangutans and white-cheeked gibbons.

Omaha's Henry Doorly Zoo, Nebraska
www.omahazoo.com/exhibits/expedition-madagascar/
Exhibition Madagascar is a huge exhibit featuring some of Madagascar's most unusual animals. Here you will see many species of lemurs, including ring-tailed and ruffed lemurs, as well as fascinating sifakas.

Websites

WWF, Great Apes
www.worldwildlife.org/species/finder/greatapes/greatapes.html
All of the world's great apes are endangered, some critically. This website looks at the threats facing them, such as habitat loss, climate change, and illegal poaching.

All about Wildlife
www.allaboutwildlife.com/rainforest-primates-monkeys-apes-and-lemurs
Find out all about the primates that live in the rainforest: from chimpanzees and gorillas to orangutans and gibbons. This website also has a list of the top 10 endangered animals and the top 10 ways you can help save wildlife.

Jungle Friends Primate Sanctuary
www.junglefriends.org/
Located in Gainesville, Florida, this sanctuary rescues monkeys from around the U.S. that have been confiscated by authorities, retired from research, or are unwanted pets.

Apes and monkeys
quiz answers

1) A	7) C
2) C	8) A
3) B	9) B
4) C	10) C
5) A	11) B
6) A	12) B